Minibeast Babies

Catherine Veitch

Raintree

Raintree is an imprint of Capstone Global Library Limited, a company incorporated in England and Wales having its registered office at 7 Pilgrim Street, London, EC4V 6LB – Registered company number: 6695582

www.raintreepublishers.co.uk
myorders@raintreepublishers.co.uk

Text © Capstone Global Library Limited 2013
First published in hardback in 2013
Paperback edition first published in 2014
The moral rights of the proprietor have been asserted.

Edited by Daniel Nunn, Rebecca Rissman, and Catherine Veitch
Designed by Cynthia Della-Rovere
Picture research by Ruth Blair
Production by Victoria Fitzgerald
Originated by Capstone Global Library
Printed and bound in China

ISBN 978 1 406 25926 1 (hardback)
17 16 15 14 13
10 9 8 7 6 5 4 3 2 1

ISBN 978 1 406 25933 9 (paperback)
18 17 16 15 14
10 9 8 7 6 5 4 3 2 1

British Library Cataloguing in Publication Data
Veitch, Catherine.
Minibeast babies. -- (Animal babies)
592.1'39-dc23
A full catalogue record for this book is available from the British Library.

Acknowledgements
We would like to thank the following for permission to reproduce photographs: Corbis pp. 9 (© Heidi & Hans-Juergen Koch/Minden Pictures); dreamstime.com p. 21 (© Halil I. Inci); Getty Images pp. 6 (Dorling Kindersley), 14 (Mark Moffett/Minden Pictures); Naturepl pp. title page (© Paul Harcourt Davies), 8 (© Martin Dohrn), 10 (© Kim Taylor), 13 (© Paul Harcourt Davies), 16 (© Meul / ARCO), 18 (© Meul / ARCO); 22 (© Simon Colmer), 23 (© Paul Harcourt Davies); Shutterstock pp. 4 (© Sim Kay Seng), 5 (© FloridaStock, © irin-k, © D. Kucharski & K. Kucharska), 7 (© photofun), 11 (© Cathy Keifer, © James Laurie), 12 (© Sue Robinson), 13 (© Torsten Dietrich), 15 (© Gherasim Rares), 17 (© kurt_G), 19 (© Dr. Morley Read), 20 (© Kletr), 22 (© vaklav, © Subbotina Anna), 23 (© Cathy Keifer, © FloridaStock).

Front cover photograph of wolf spider mother with spiderlings reproduced with kind permission of Shutterstock (© kurt_G).

We would like to thank Michael Bright for his invaluable help in the preparation of this book.

Every effort has been made to contact copyright holders of material reproduced in this book. Any omissions will be rectified in subsequent printings if notice is given to the publisher.

Contents

What is a minibeast?

dragonfly

A minibeast is a small animal or creepy crawly.

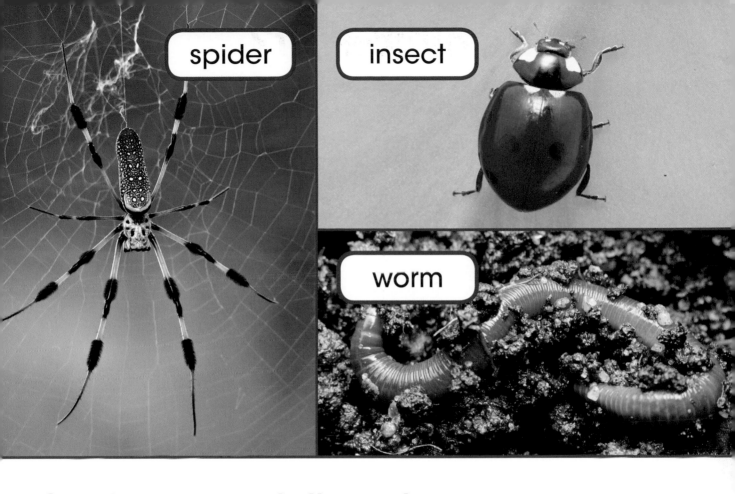

spider

insect

worm

Spiders are minibeasts.

Insects and worms are minibeasts.

How are baby minibeasts born?

eggs

Many minibeasts lay eggs.
Some minibeasts lay eggs on soil.

eggs

Some minibeasts lay eggs on leaves.

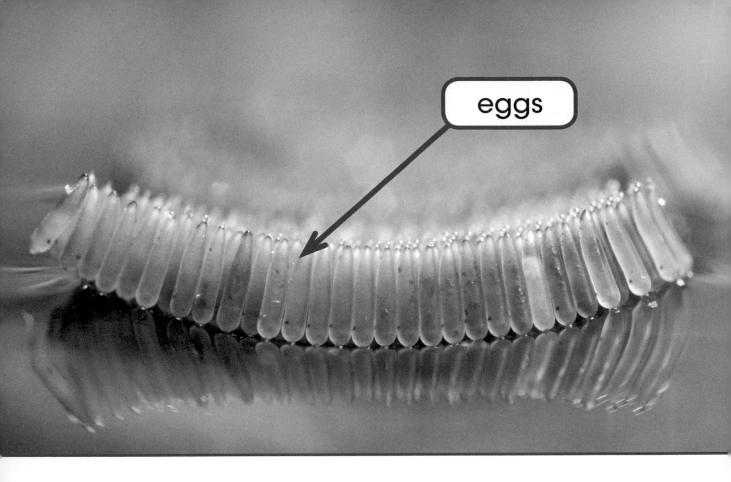

eggs

Some minibeasts lay eggs on water.

eggs

Some minibeasts lay eggs on food.

larvae

egg

Larvae can hatch from eggs.

larva

parent

Larvae do not look like their parents.

nymph

Nymphs can hatch from eggs.

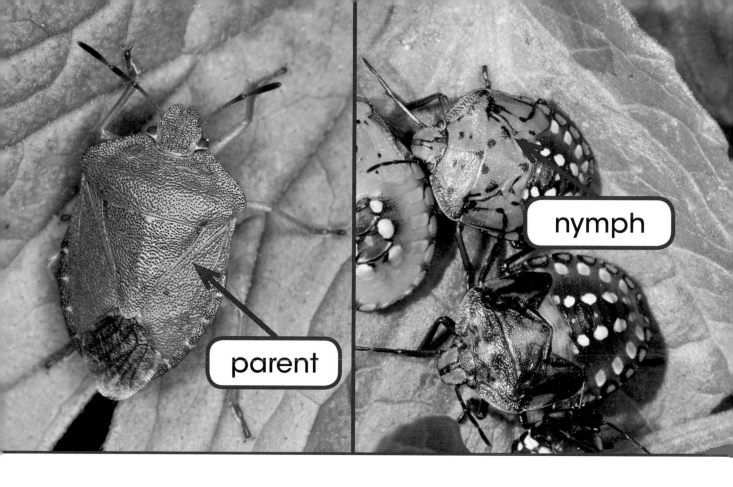

parent

nymph

Nymphs look like their parents.

Caring for baby minibeasts

Some minibeasts care for
their babies.

larvae

These worker bees bring food to their larvae.

This ant carries its baby to
a safe place.

babies

This spider carries its babies on its back.

Growing up

Many minibeast babies look after themselves. Some feed on smaller minibeasts.

Some feed on plants.

Some minibeasts find a new home.

They hide from predators.

Life cycle of a minibeast

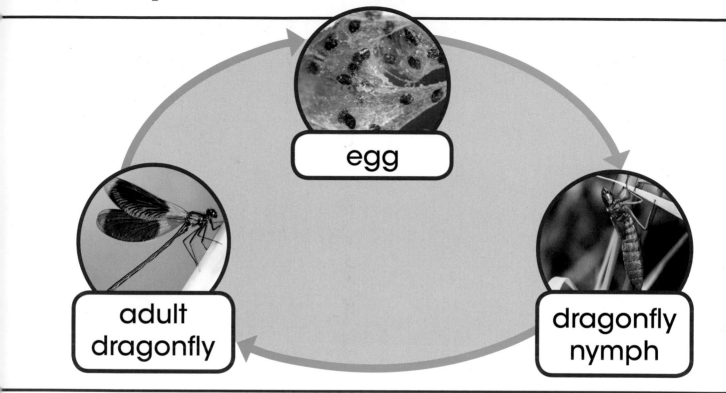

egg

adult dragonfly

dragonfly nymph

A life cycle shows the different stages of an animal's life. This is the life cycle of a dragonfly.

Picture glossary

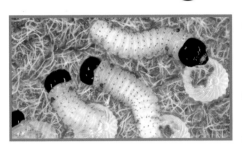

larva stage some minibeasts have when they first hatch. More than one is larvae.

nymph stage some minibeasts have when they first hatch

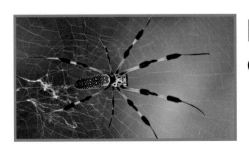

predator animal that eats other animals

Index

Notes for parents and teachers

Before reading

Show children a collection of photos and videos of minibeasts. National Geographic and BBC Nature are useful websites. Explain what a minibeast is and discuss the characteristics of minibeasts.

After reading

- Mount photos of adult and baby minibeasts on card, and play games of snap and pairs where the children have to match a baby minibeast with its parent. Model the correct pairs first.

- Ask children to label the parts of a minibeast: for example, wings, head, legs, antennae.

- Look at page 22 and discuss the life cycle stages of a minibeast. Mount photos of the egg, nymph and adult stages and ask children to put the photos in order. Encourage children to draw a life cycle of a human to compare. Compare how different minibeasts care for their babies. Discuss the care human babies need.

- Some children will be curious to learn the names of the minibeasts. Therefore, to extend children's knowledge, the minibeasts are as follows: dragonfly: p4; spider, ladybird, worm: p5; snail eggs: p6; butterfly eggs: p7; mosquito eggs: p8; housefly: p9; cabbage white butterfly larvae and eggs: p10; monarch butterfly larvae and eggs, monarch butterfly: p11; green shield bug nymphs: p12; green shield bug parent and nymphs: p13; earwig: p14; worker bees and larvae: p15; yellow mound ant with pupa: p16; wolf spider and spiderlings: p17; ladybird larvae: p18; caterpillar: p19; wasp spiderlings: p20; caterpillar: p21.